A HOLE IN THE WHOLE

ELEONORA MARTON

A FRECKLE
ON THE CHEEK

A PIECE OF FLUFF
ON A SLEEVE

A GRAIN OF SAND
ON THE TOWEL

A MARBLE
IN THE SAND

A WORRY
IN MY MIND

A PIECE OF CONFETTI
ON THE GROUND

THE MOON
IN THE NIGHT

THE BUTTON
ON MY CUFF

A BUG
ON A LEAF

OUR PLACE
IN SPACE

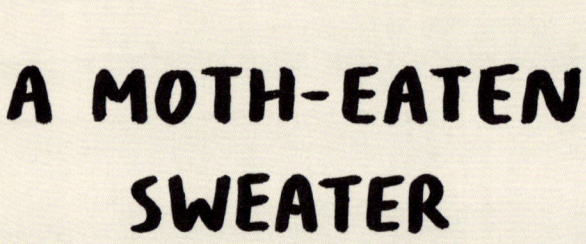

A MOTH-EATEN
SWEATER

A PILL
IN MY PALM

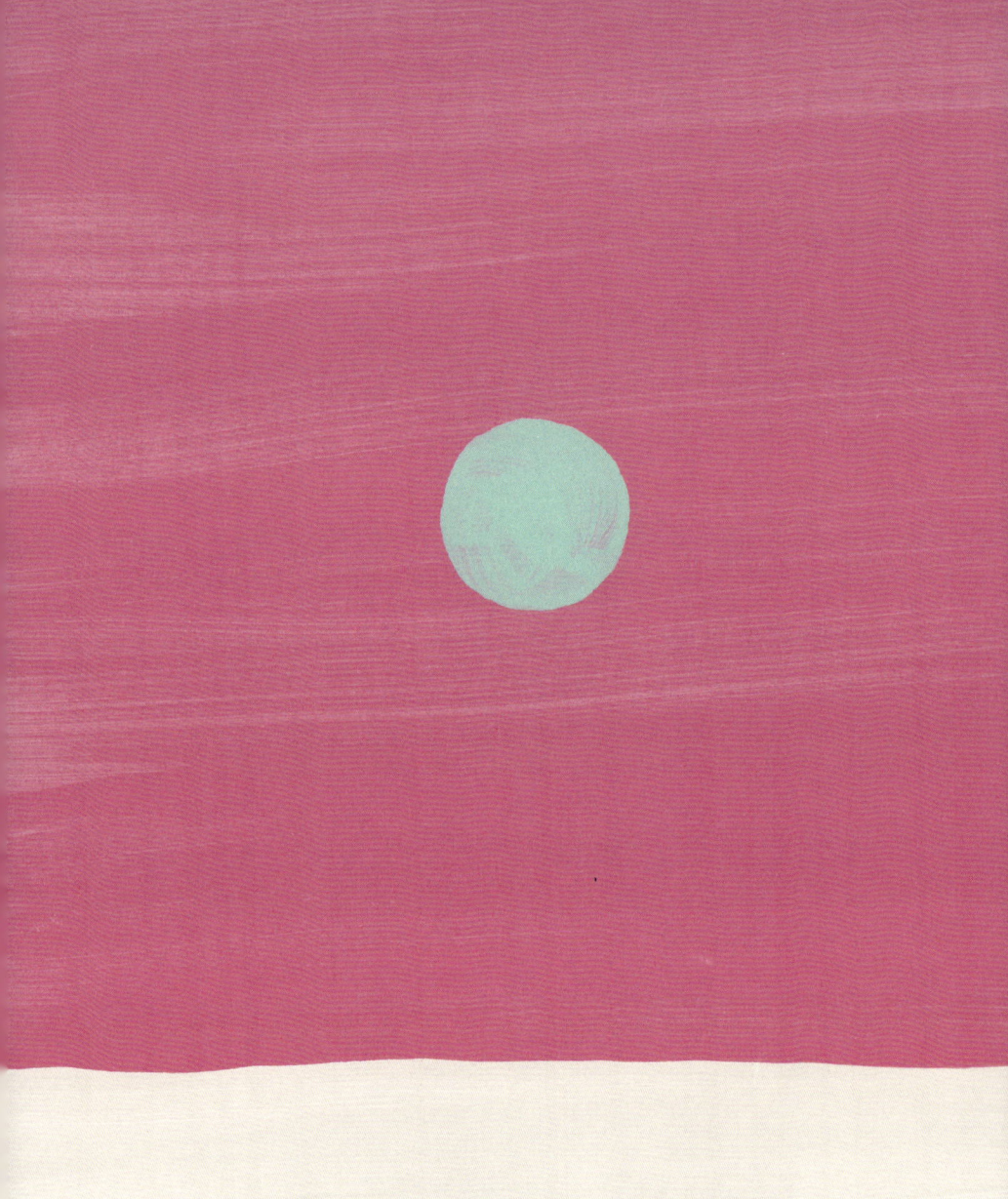

A LOOSE MINT
IN MY PURSE

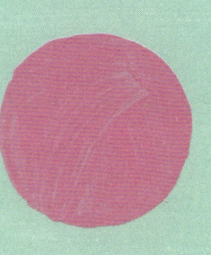

A PAINT DROP
ON THE FLOOR

THE NUMBER ONE
ON A DICE

A HOLE
IN THE WHOLE

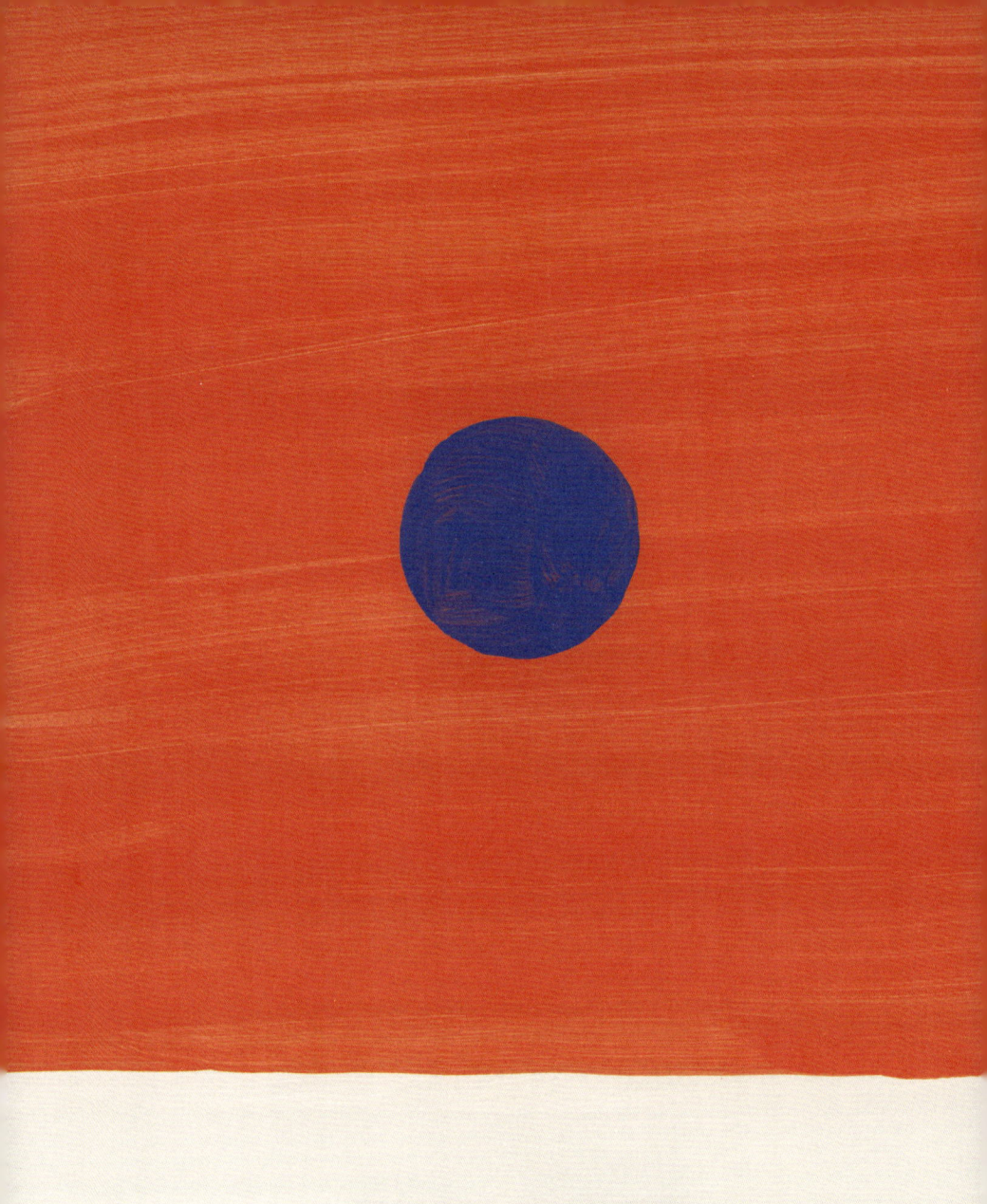

THE HEAD
OF A NAIL

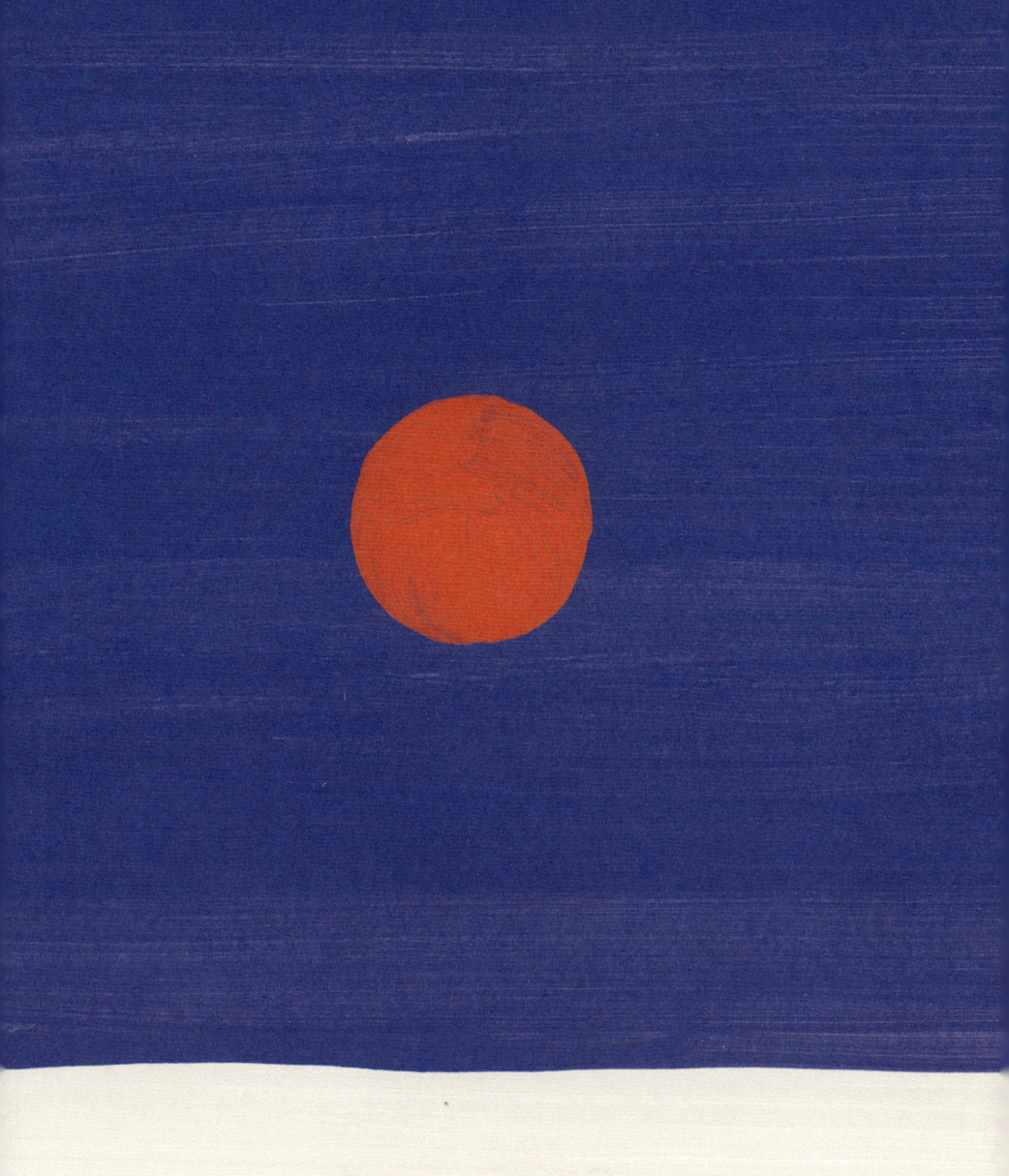

THE COIN
IN MY POCKET

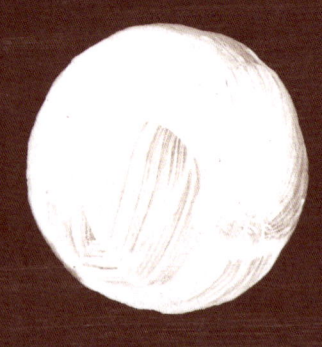

A MARSHMALLOW
IN MY COCOA

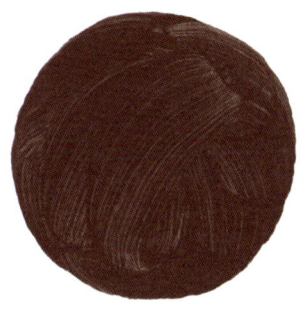

A DOG POO
IN THE SNOW

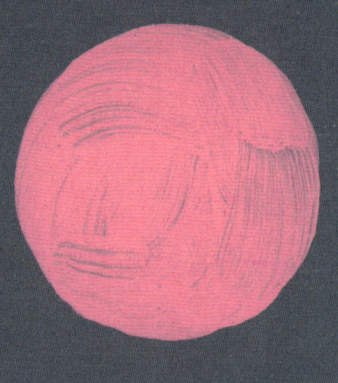

GUM
UNDER MY SHOE

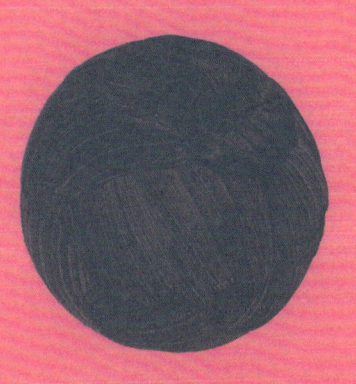

A STONE
IN MY SHOE

THE FIRST RAINDROP
ON THE GROUND

THE LAST BISCUIT
ON A PLATE

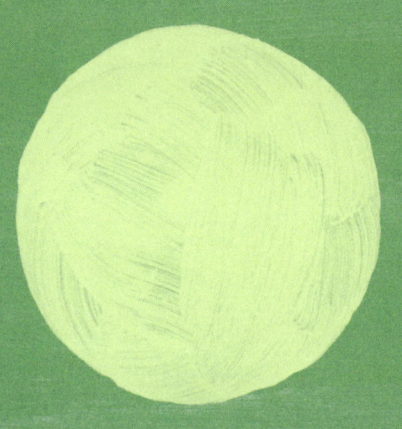

A POTATO
IN THE PEA SOUP

A PEA
IN THE POTATO SOUP

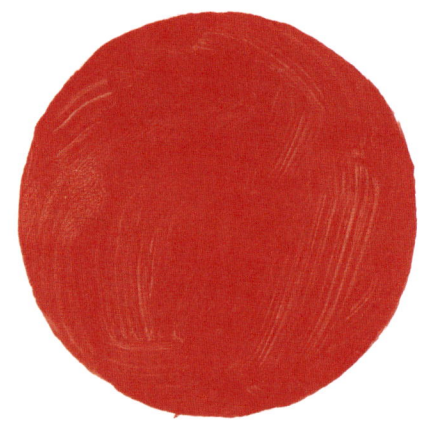

THE FOCAL POINT
OF THIS PAGE

A CANDY
ON MY TONGUE

A PIE
IN THE SKY

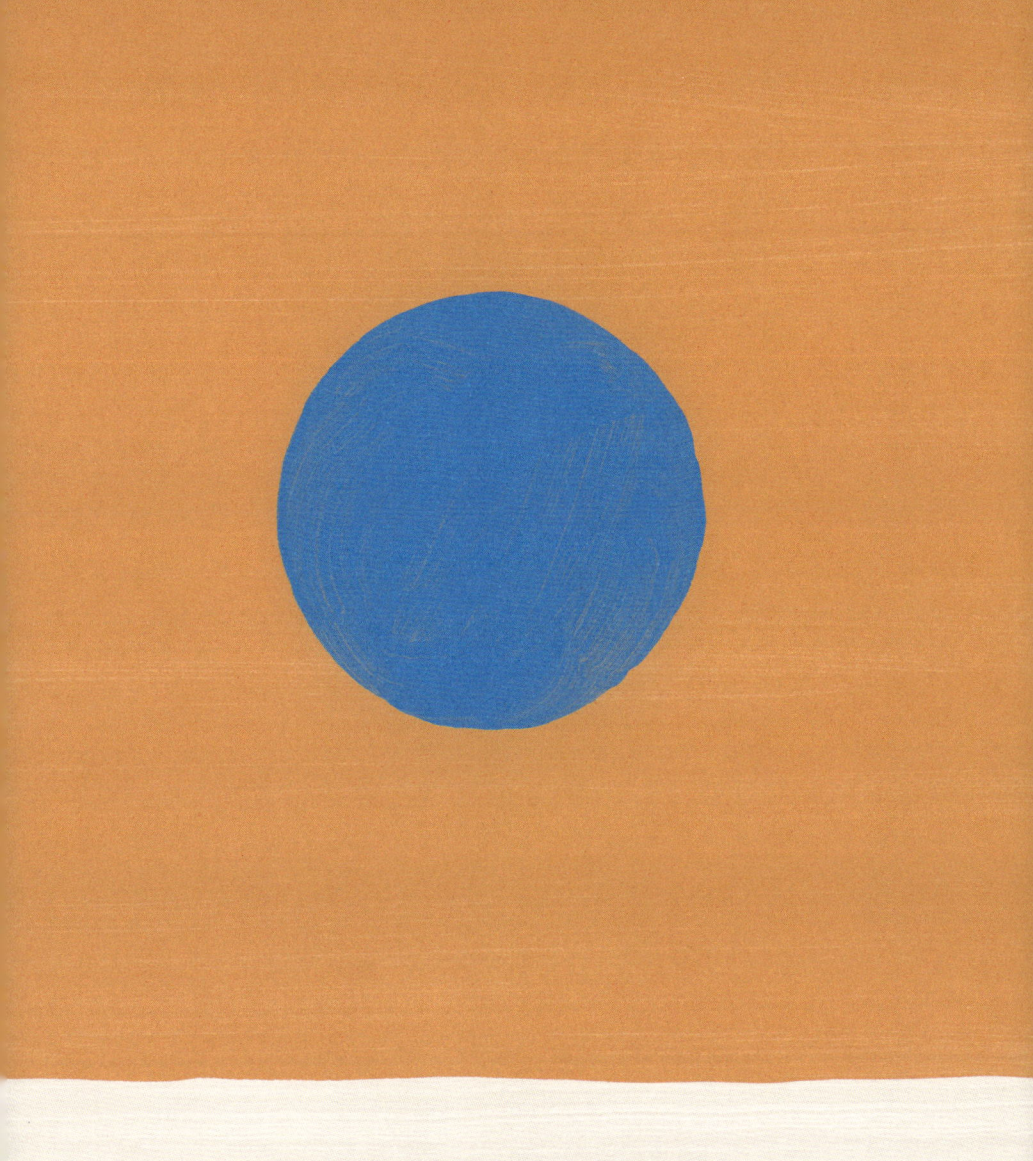

AN UMBRELLA
AT THE BEACH

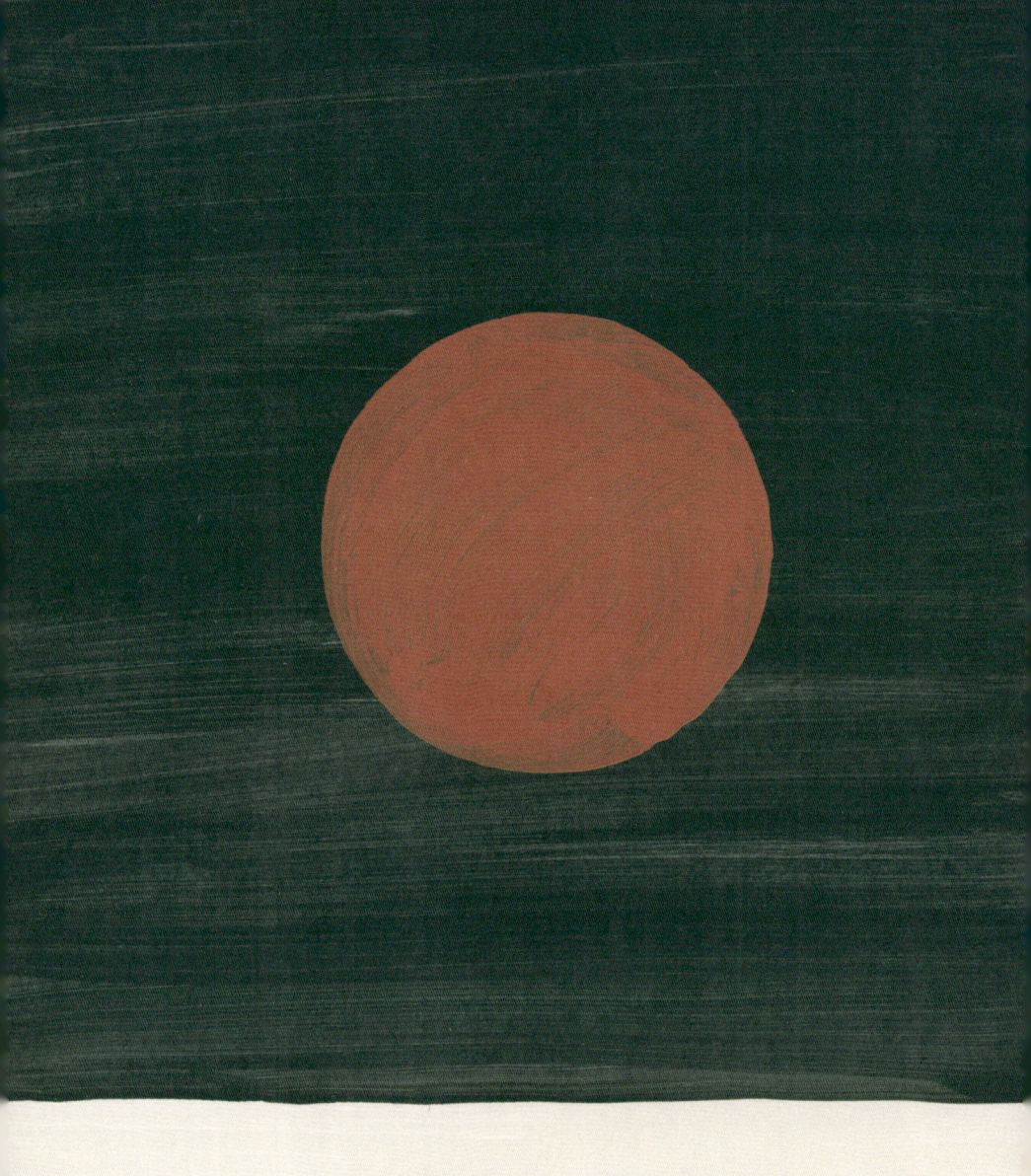

A TREE STUMP
IN THE WOODS

A GAP
IN THE FENCE

THE KNOB
OF YOUR DOOR

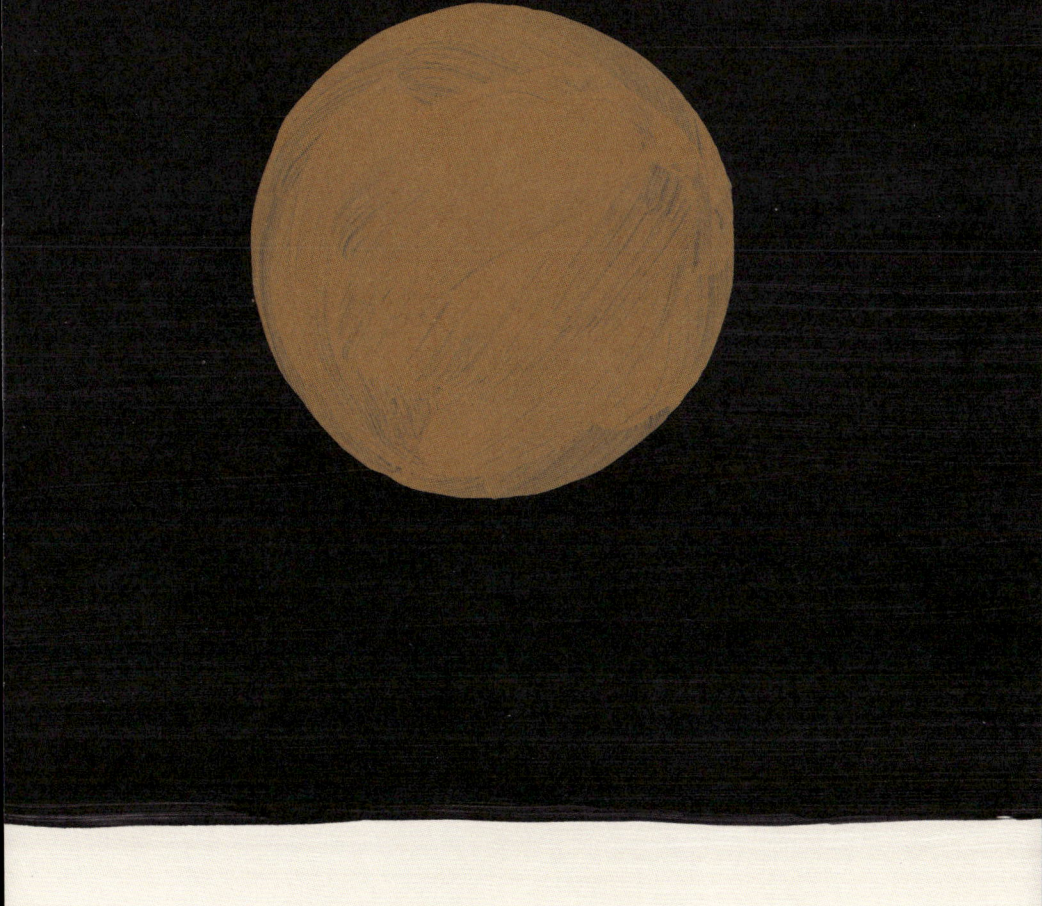

YOUR DOOR
FROM MY PEEPHOLE

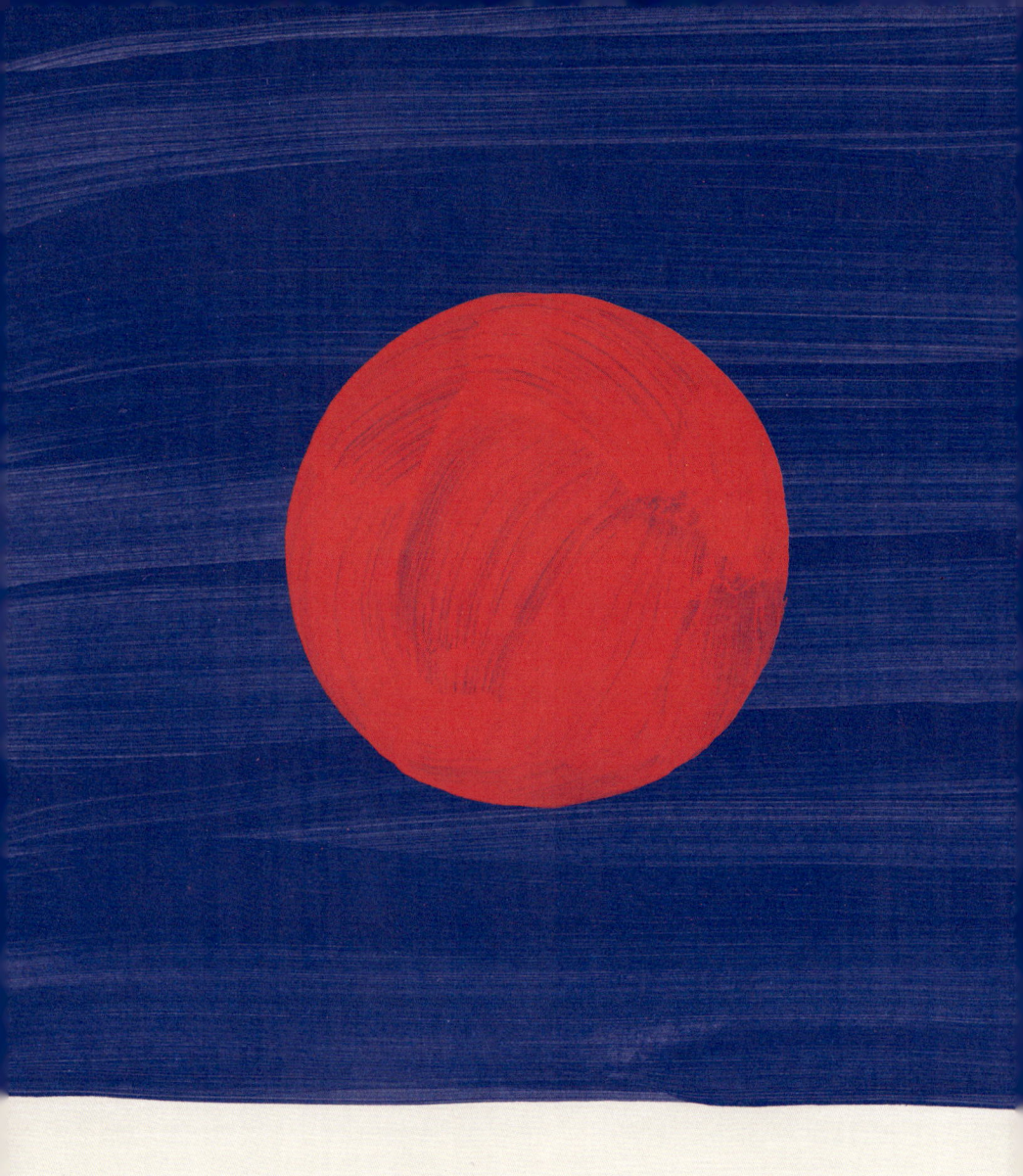

THE STOP BUTTON
ON THE MACHINE

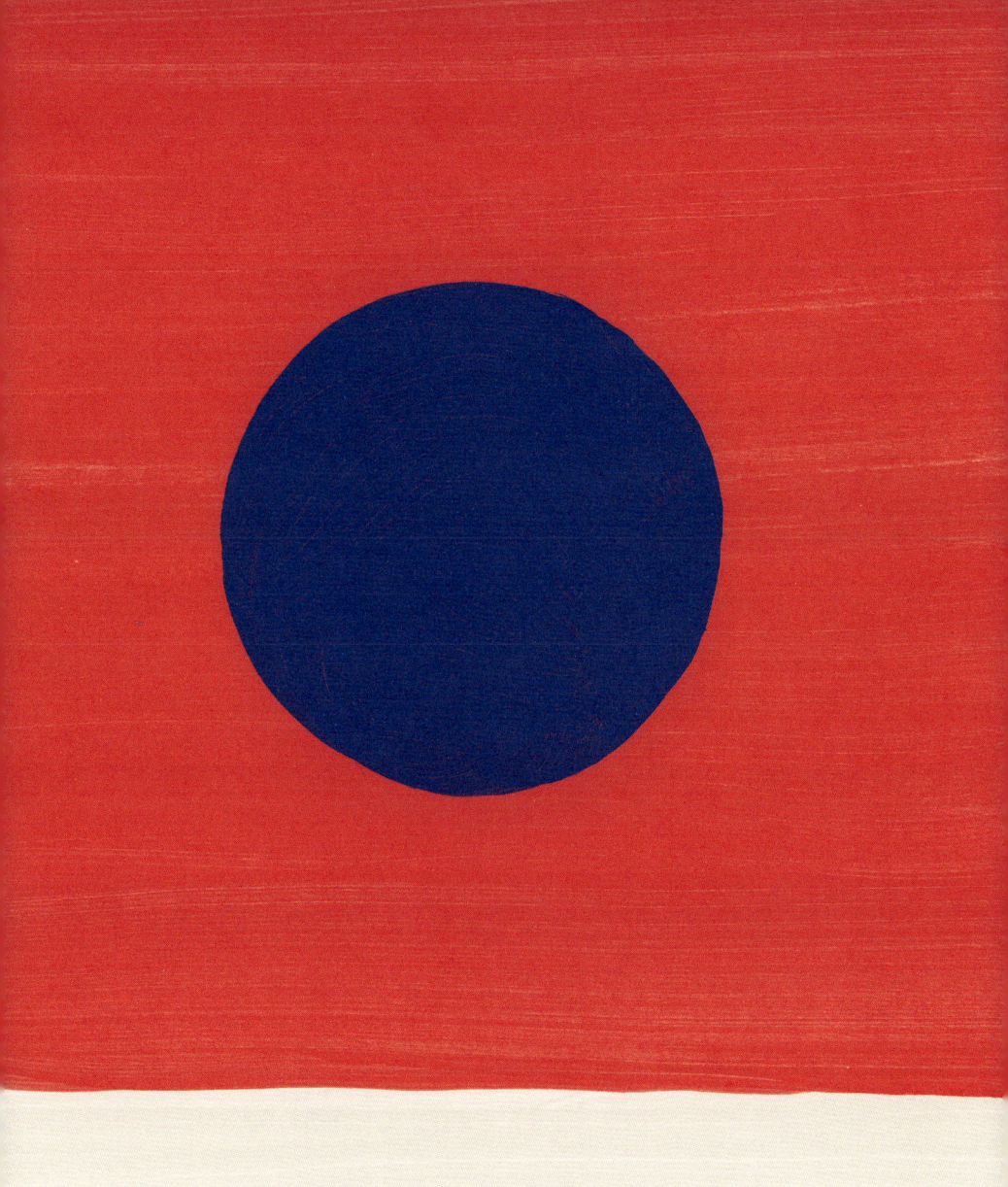

A BLUE CIRCLE
ON A RED SQUARE

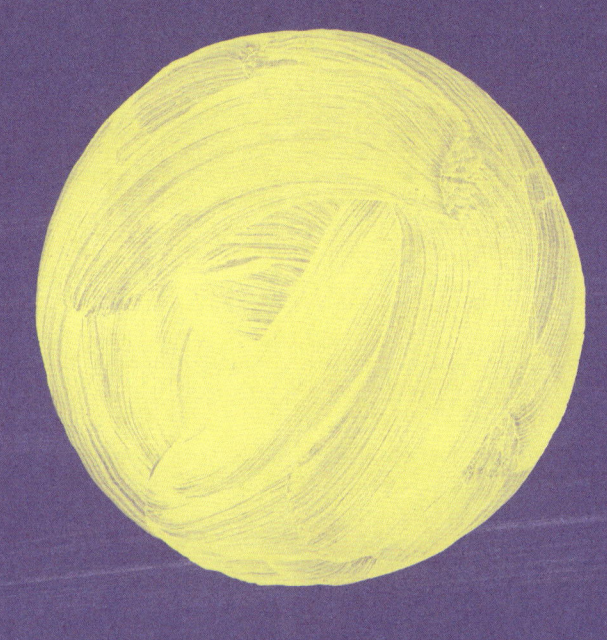

A CIRCLE
IN THE FOREGROUND

A CIRCLE
IN THE BACKGROUND

A NEST
IN THE TREE

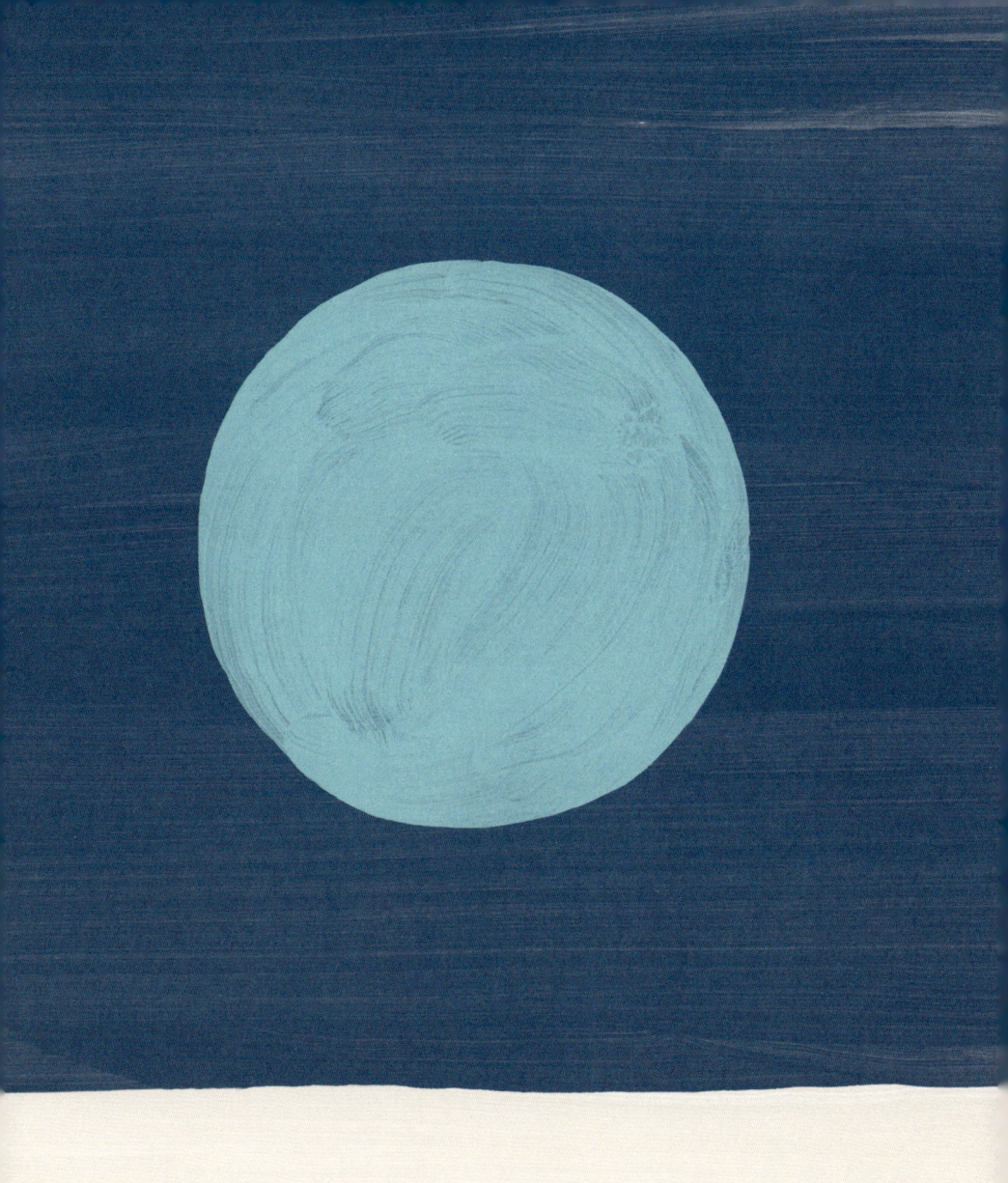

AN EGG
IN THE NEST

THE ENTRANCE
TO THE TUNNEL

THE LIGHT AT
THE END OF THE TUNNEL

THE PUPIL
OF YOUR EYE

THE SKY
THROUGH MY EYE

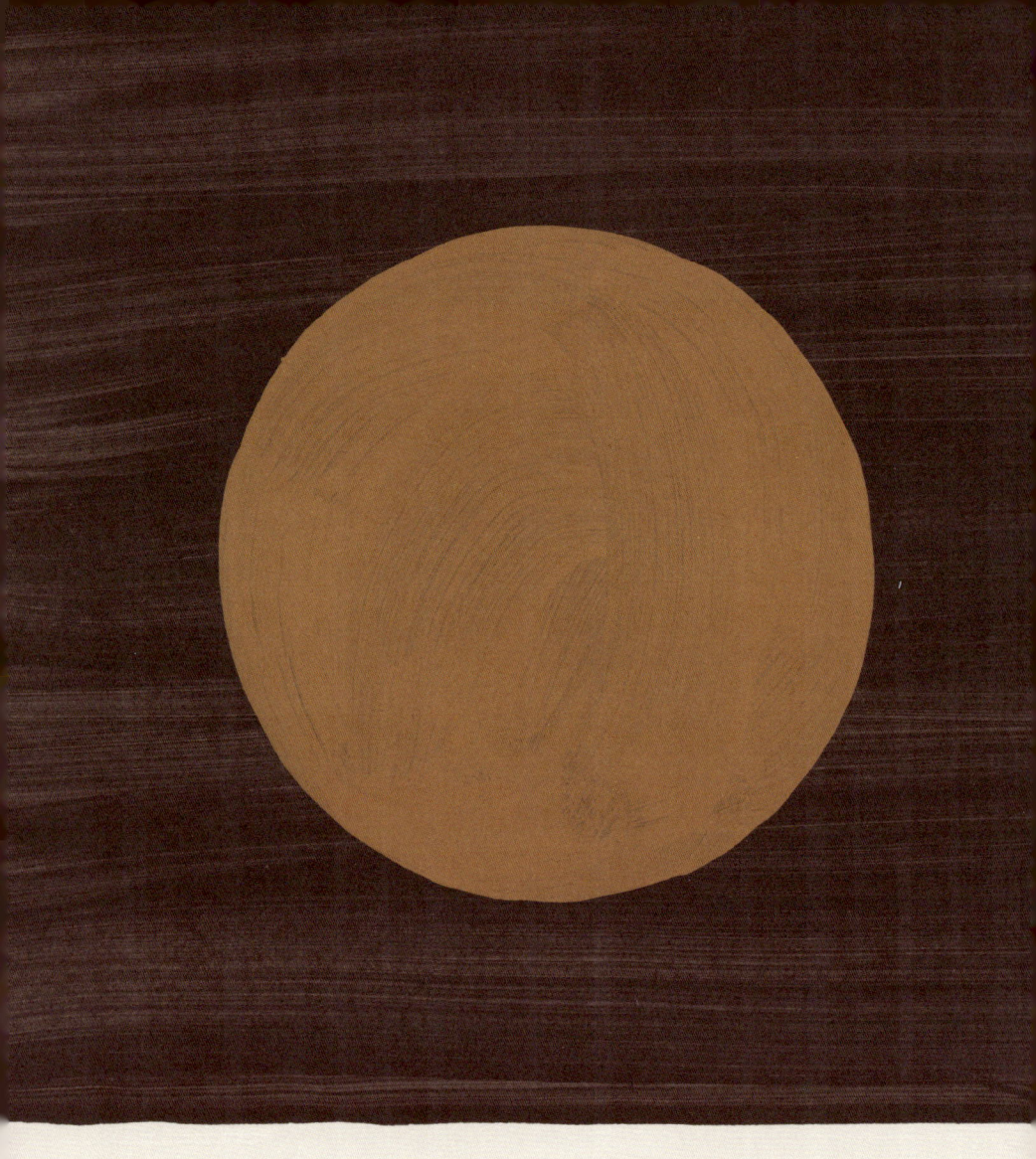

A WATER MARK
ON THE TABLE

THE CHIP
IN A COOKIE

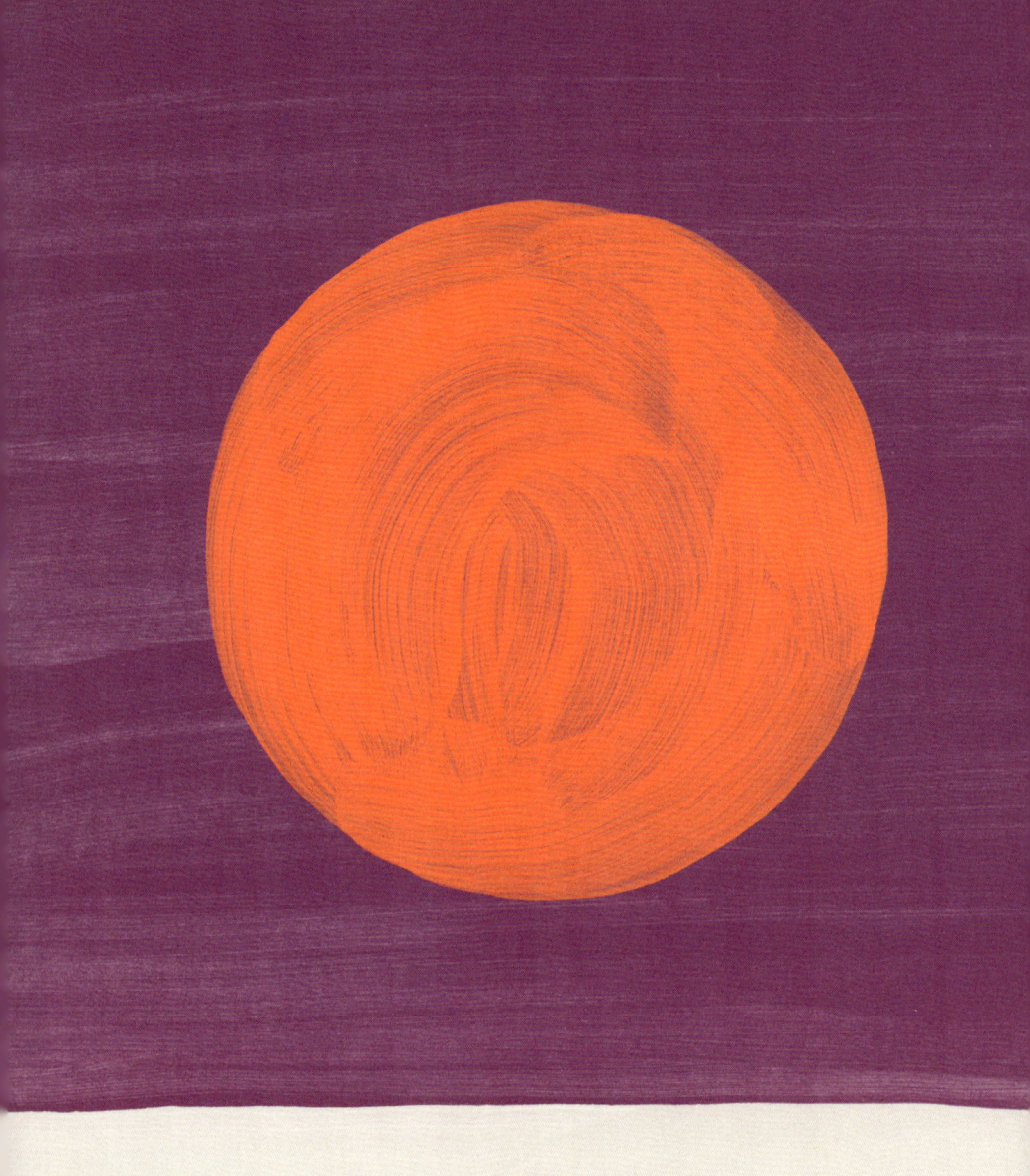

THE OUTSIDE
FROM INSIDE

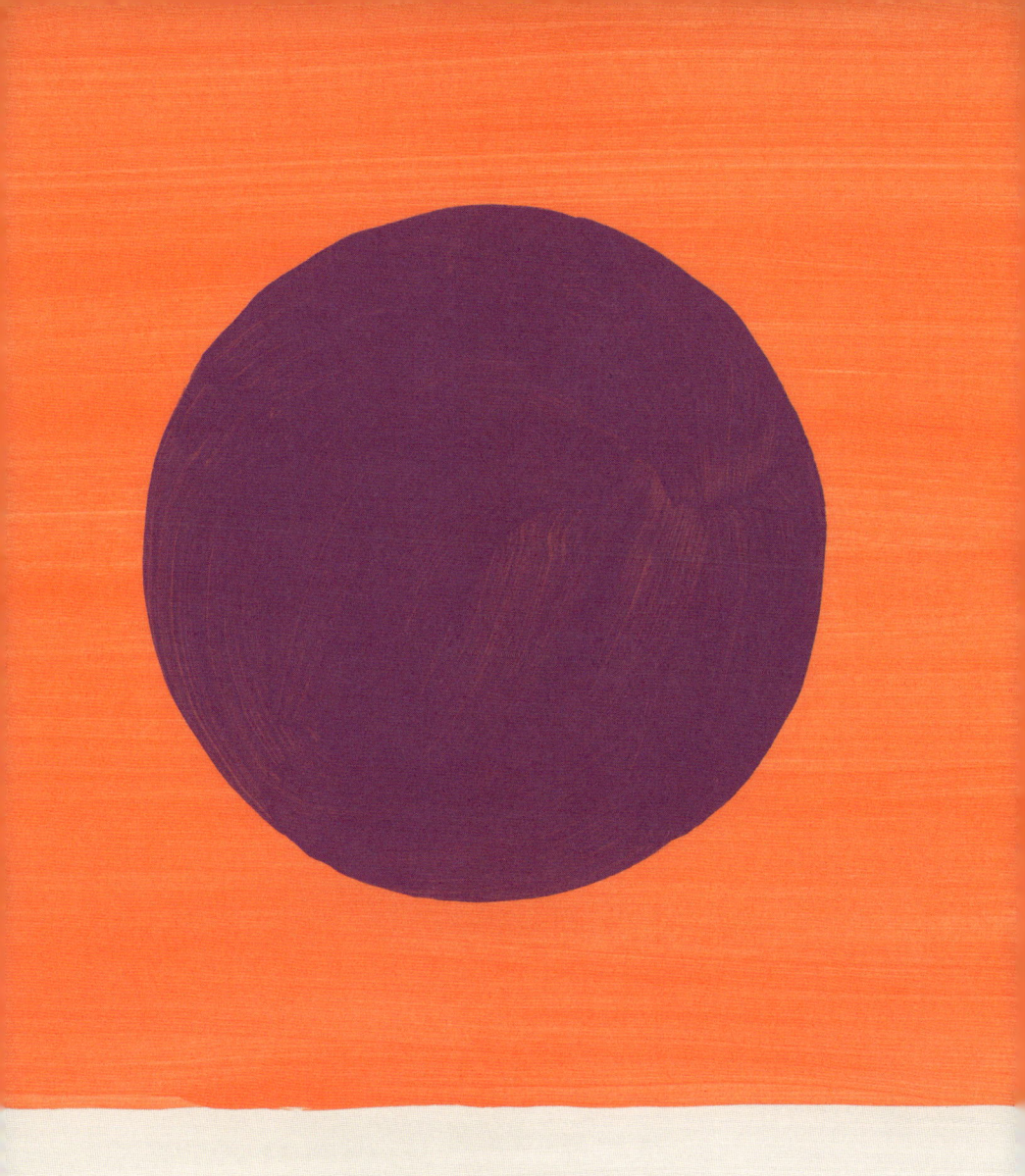

THE INSIDE
FROM OUTSIDE

THE SUN
THROUGH SHADES

THE SHADE
IN THE HEAT

A CUT OUT
CIRCLE

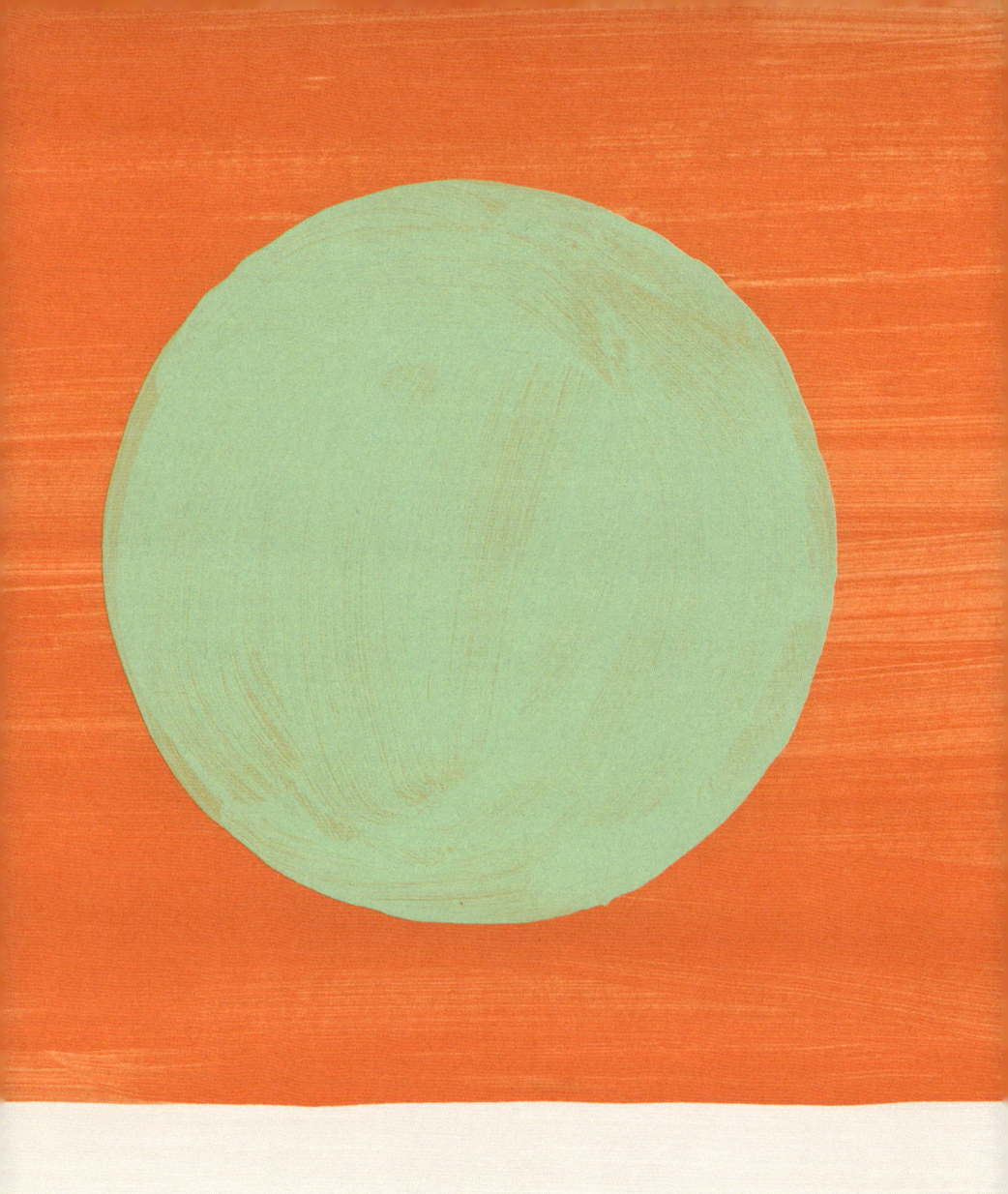

A STUCK ON
CIRCLE

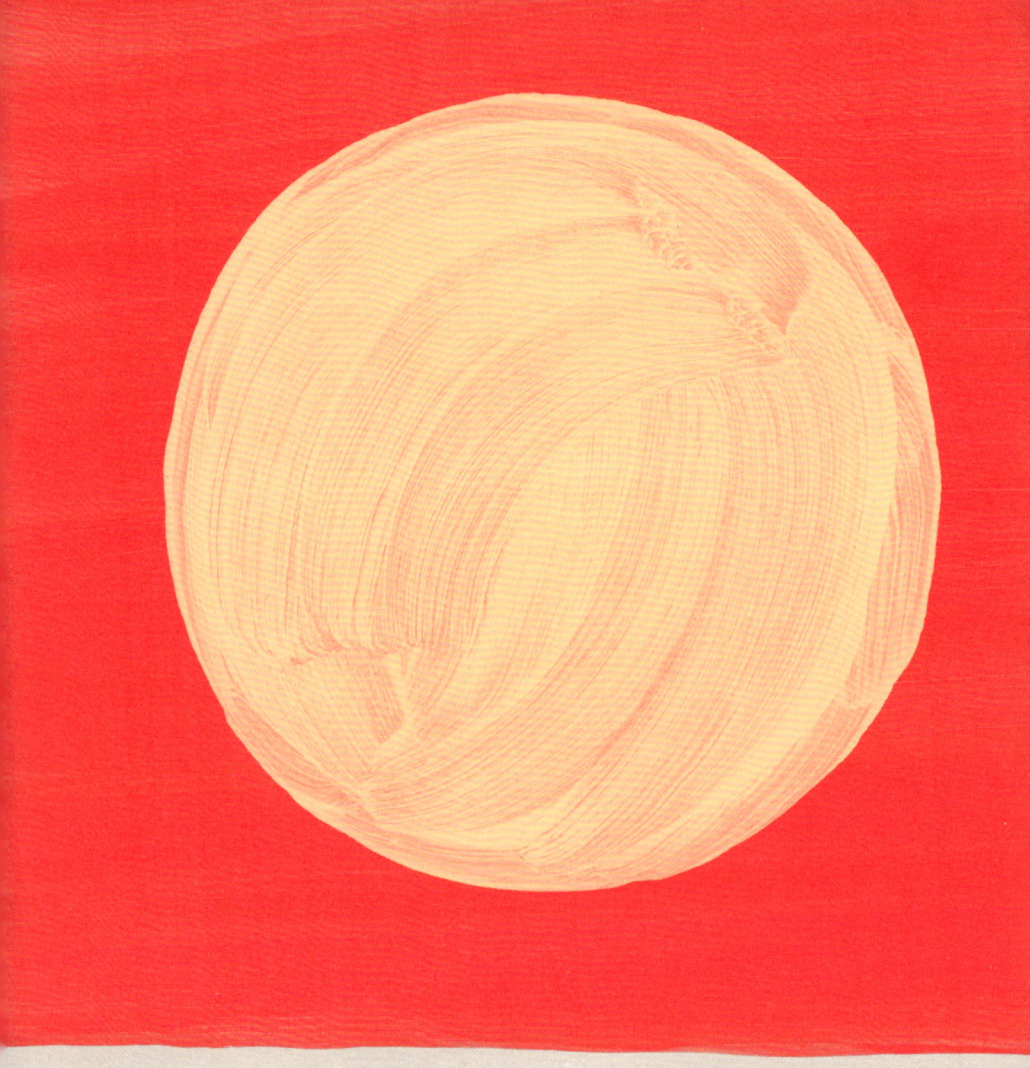

A PIMPLE
READY TO SQUEEZE

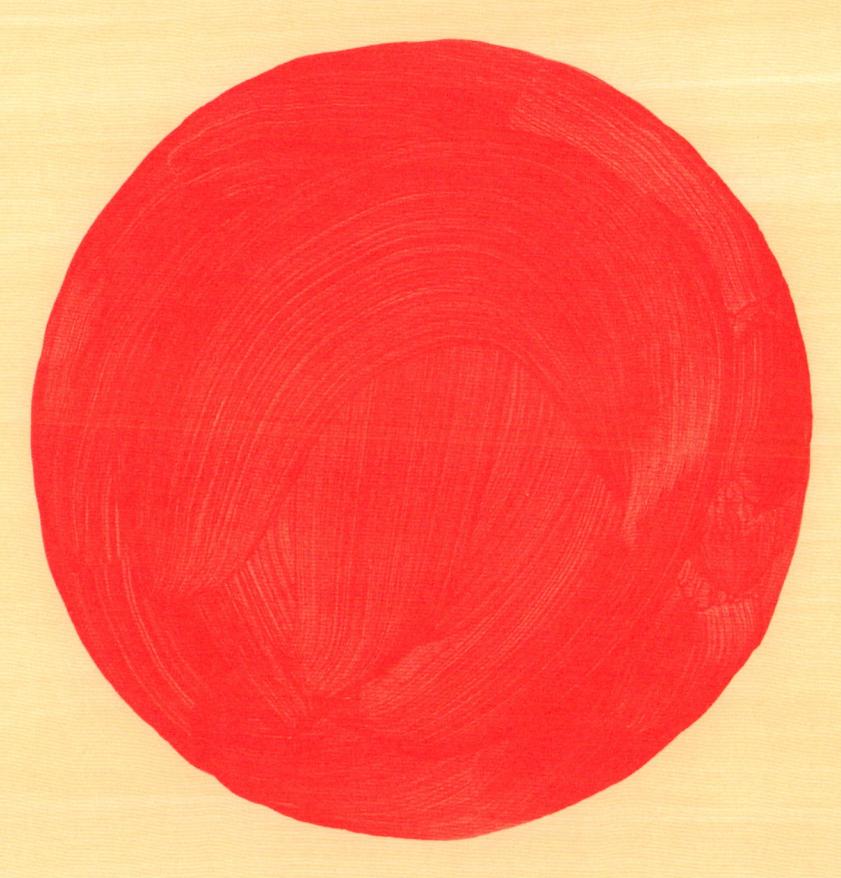

A BRUISE
ON THE KNEE

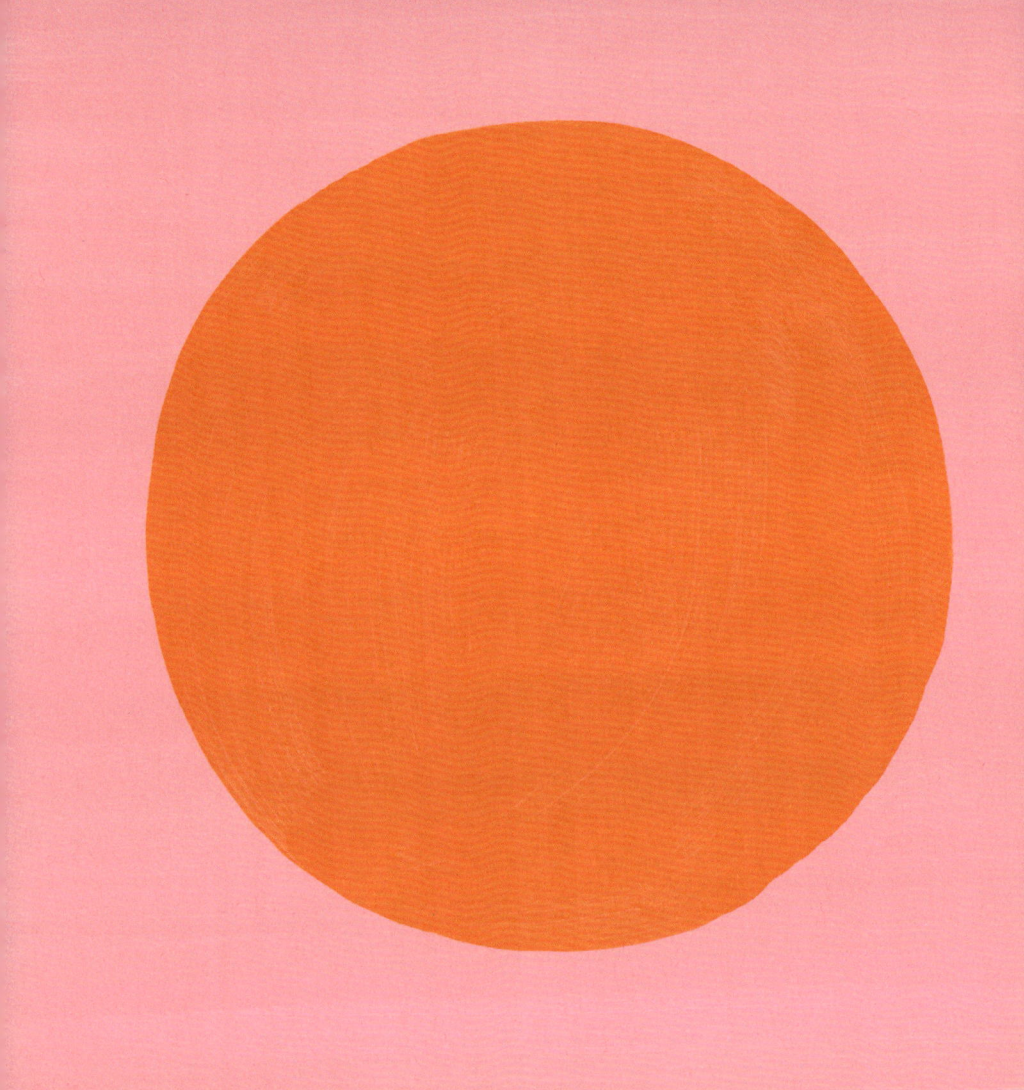

THE BEST HOUR
OF THE DAY

THE POINT
OF THE STORY

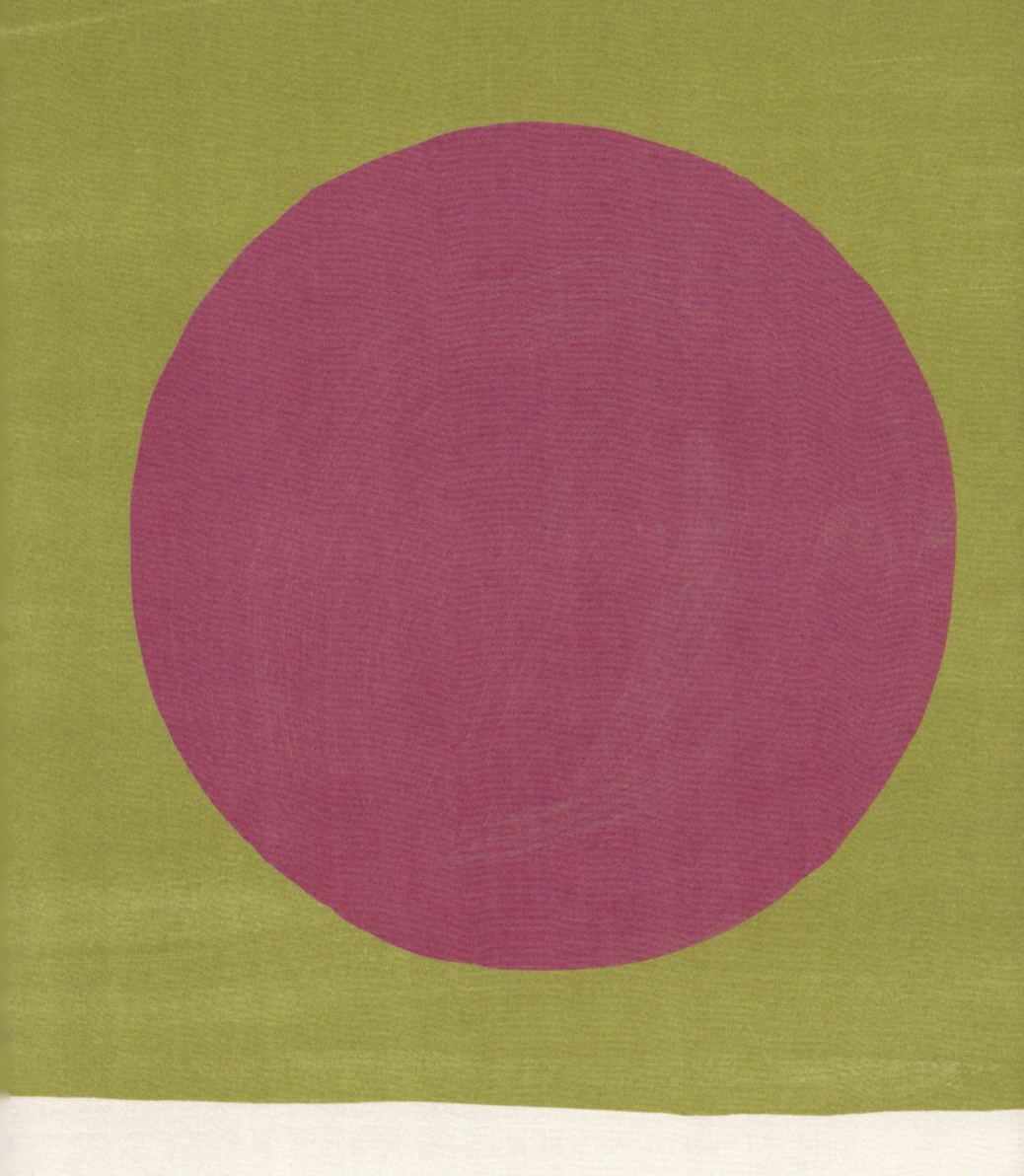

A MEMORY
IN YOUR MIND

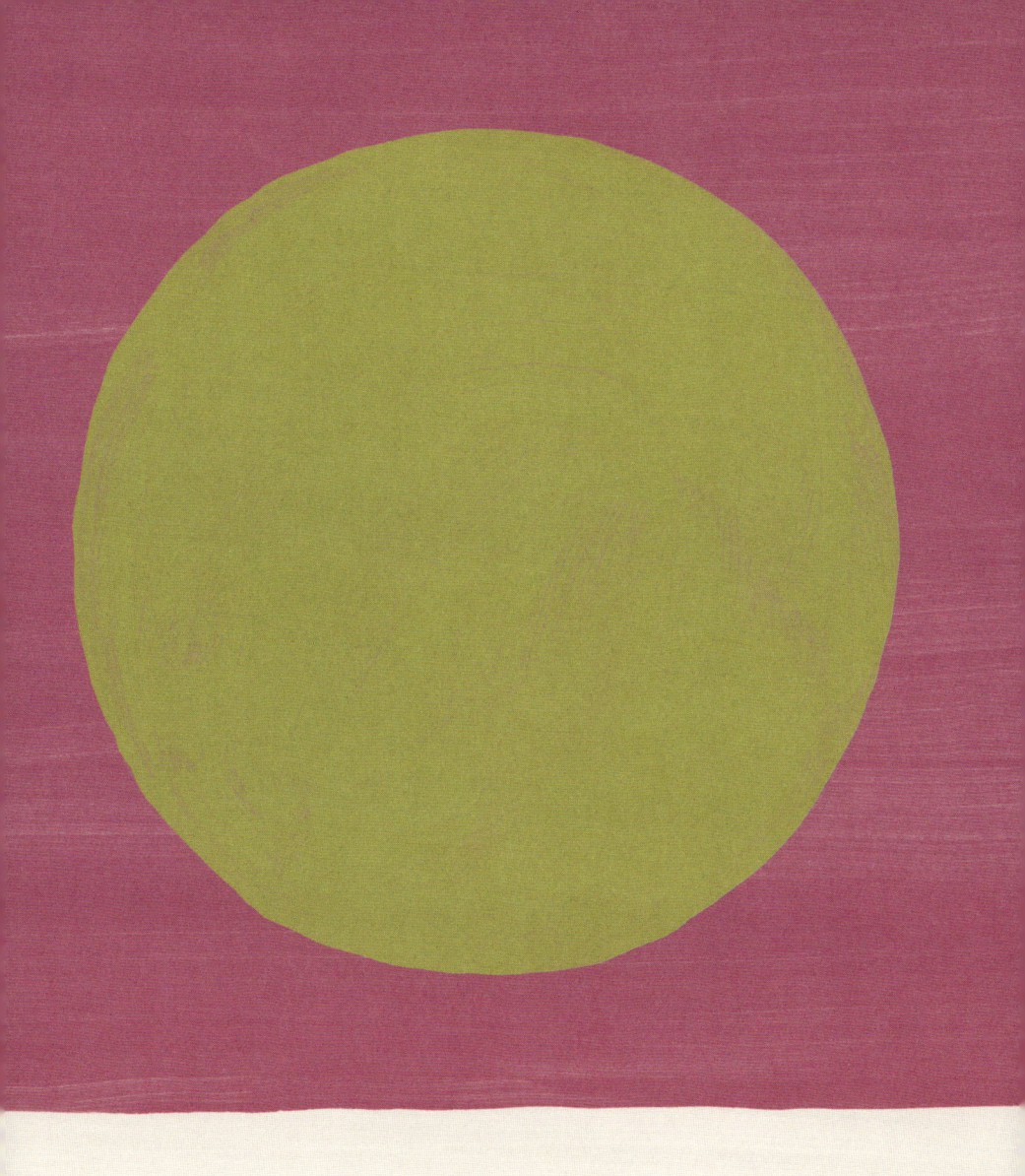

A DREAM
IN MY MIND

A BALLOON
FLOATING IN THE AIR

THE AIR
IN THE BALLOON

THE START
OF SOMETHING

THE END
OF SOMETHING

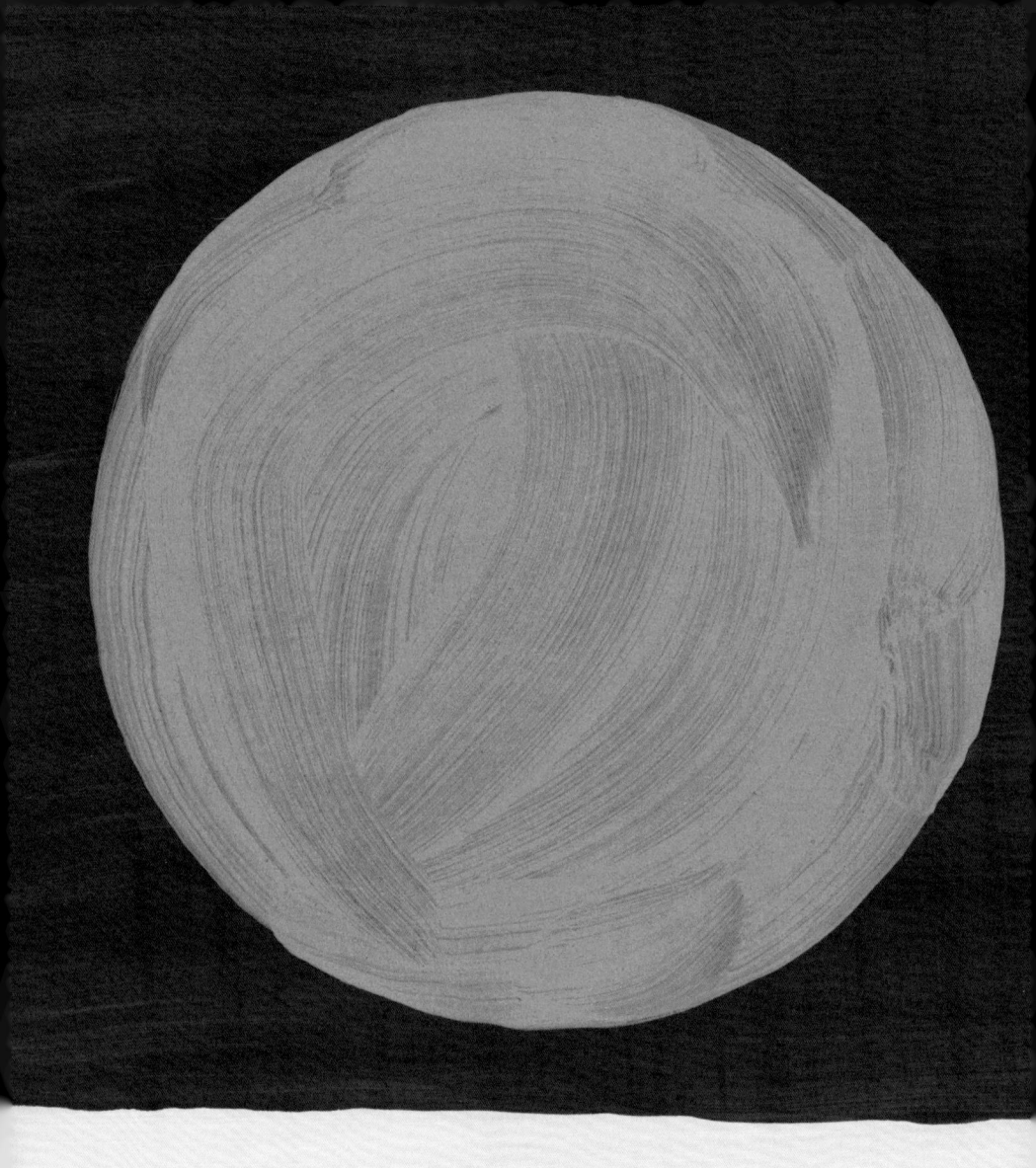

A MINUTE
OF YOUR TIME

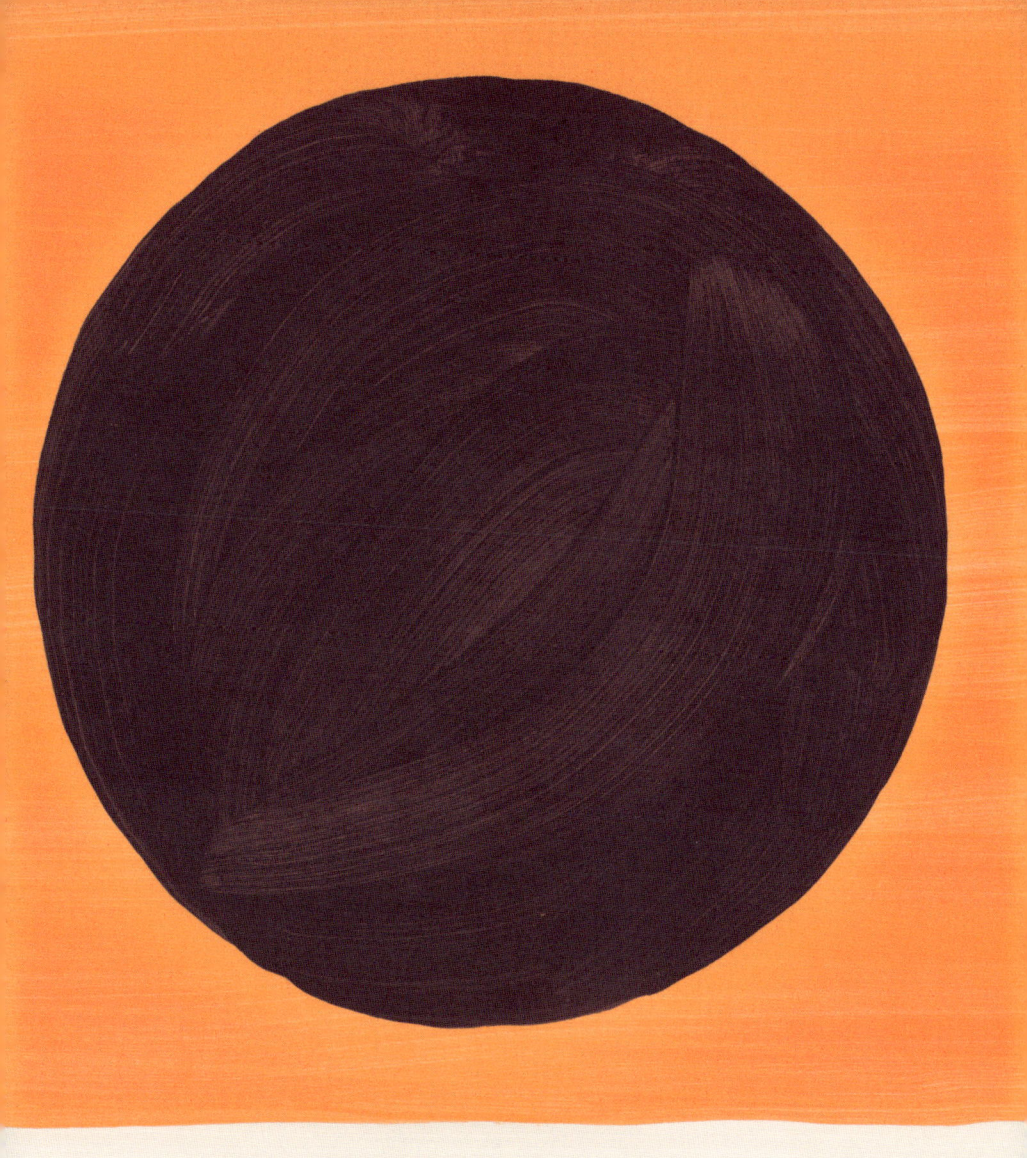

THE SPOT
YOU MISSED

THE SOUND
IN THE ROOM

THE SONG
IN MY EAR

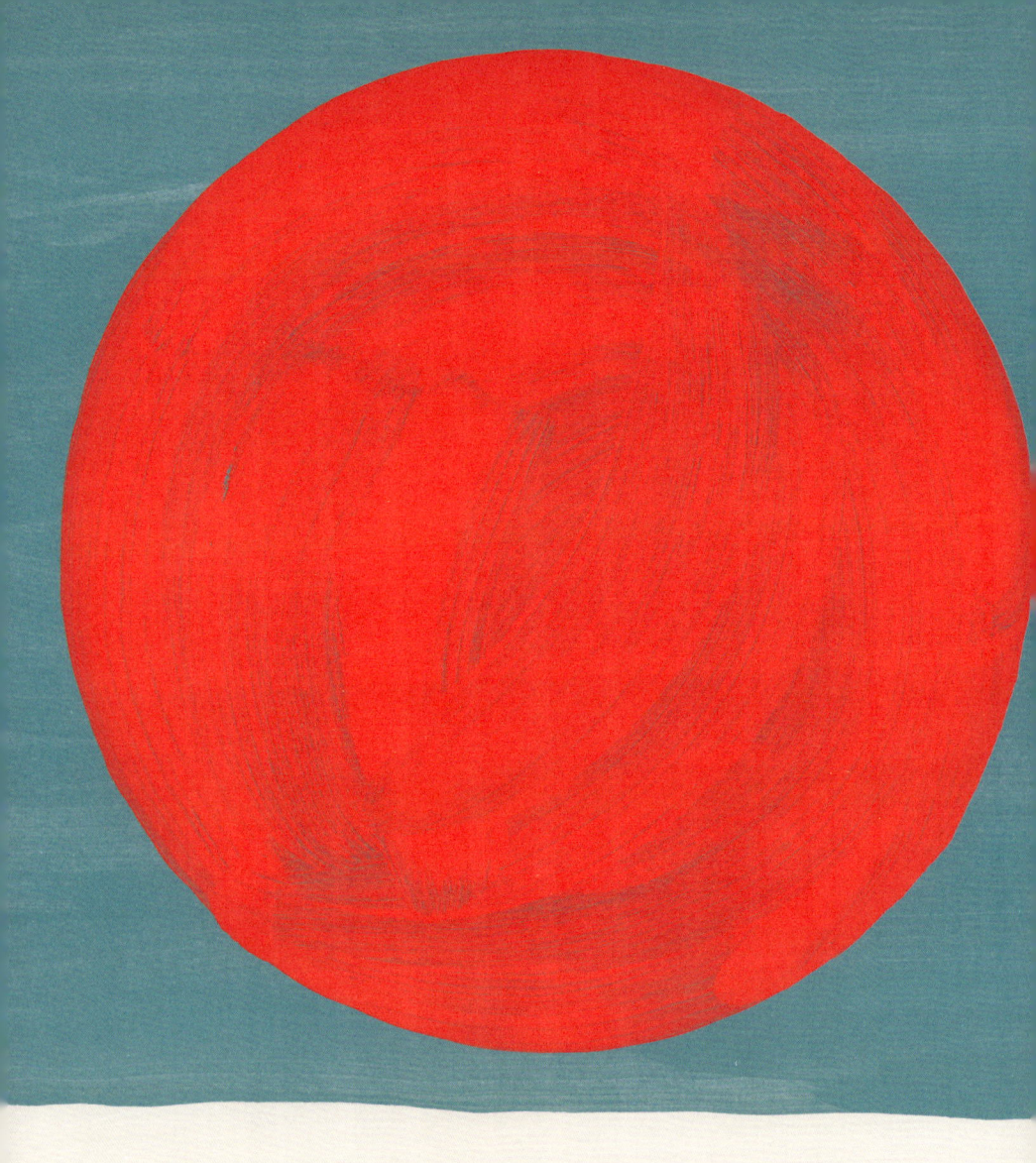

ANOTHER WORRY
IN MY MIND

THE BALL
IN YOUR COURT

A CLOCK REMOVED
FROM THE WALL

A STEAMY MIRROR ON THE WALL

THE BRIGHT
SIDE

THE FLIP
SIDE

A BIG CIRCLE
IN A SMALL SPACE

AN INVISIBLE CIRCLE ON THE PAGE